the
way
of
things.

old new poems
joshua dov.

for you.
the light that guides
the rock that grounds

the
way
of
things.

table of contents.

american standard.

And so,
i return to where it all began
as some lonesome traveler
like kerouac and cassidy
like butch and the kid
running away
to simply
catch up to where i left off.
i am the struggle
i am the fighter
i am the dreamer
i am
        the struggle.
with callous hands
and a bad back,
i try to find my keys
cause the job starts at 3
and i'm running late.
it's only been 2 weeks of work
yet it feels like a lifetime.
i been running hard all these years
against conforming
against the masses
against settling
but it has caught up to me
in the last lap of the race.
And so,
i return to the start
daylight savings ends
grey fills these days,
black fills these nights,
but the standards remain the same
on this continuing road
just as i thought they would.

love stays
within and yet
still without
and
i miss your voice.
while the morning rain
settles itself
as a sad song
for the pure
of heart and mind.

a new york city morning

the sex
last night
was good
yet
sitting here,
    alone
with the windows open
on a grey morning in may
is even better.
i got a cup of cold coffee
some fresh o.j.
bread
toasted with butter
coltrane on the radio
and
a smoke behind my ear.
this
is
it.
this
is what
they talk about,
and god damn its good.
i avoid the hustle of the outside world,
that's my hustle
twenty five years and counting.
there's nothing to prove
to them
or the rest of 'em.
and the new york times
says
all is well in

love and war
(for today that is.)
so i hold on to whatever sticks
light my smoke
and simply
get through these days.
neither poet nor pauper
but
desperately
trying to be both
or just
somewhere in between.

A / B / C

and the clock turns its hands to 3 a.m.
and my friend says goodnight
to the day
yet i stay awake
to welcome what is to come
in these wee hours of morning
maybe nothing
maybe something
maybe a little genius (ness)
but i'm still trying to learn the abc's
of life,
drunk and stoned
and i still try,
running out of excuses
searching for reasons
on a cold november evening
in new york city.
the wine was good tonight,
warming the soul like fire
as sweet jazz played in the background.
this bohemian paradise
is only getting better, i realize.
while the clock ticks,
i sit back and
smoke my smoke,
that's what i do best.
and on this friday night
a man on 86th street
preached of God
preached of love,
of hate, of kindness, of humility
and he raised his hands into the air
yearning to be saved

and i looked up
and saw a plane pass over head
and i thought of a girl
i thought of love
i thought of hate
i thought of holding her in my arms
smelling her hair
i thought of humility, all that jazz.
then the man was silent
he closed his book,
proceeding on his journey
and i fell silent
undisturbed
on the corner of 86th and Broadway.
the red neon lights flash don't walk
a taxi cab passes by
and i cross the street
feeling alone once again,
these people pass by me
all strangers,
despair on their faces
and i wonder what's on my face
besides the bitter wind
and never ending avenues.
4 a.m. rolls around
and with nothing to do
and no place to go
i end this here.

3 to 1

i've got a chip on my shoulder
that won't stop bleeding
words that can't come out
promises that can't be kept
and
dawn approaches
while the kids are still running
in the playground
of these vast city walls.
i made it home
without a scratch,
or a nod
while
silence eats away at me
breaking me down
like some sort of cancer.
praying that the wind
continues to pass through
my open windows,
it has become my armor
in the days of late,
defense against the opposition,
a shield for my heart.
and
the odds seem to be against me
three to one
but it could be worse.
so here it is
two a.m.
desperate for a friend,
hoping for a little luck
just to ease

the nerves
            quaking in my soul.
and
the angels
never had it this good
but
nothing is ever
as it seems.

front page news

it doesn't sound too good
this whole idea of war.
now,
maybe i'm a stranger
to all the worlds
politics and policies
trade sanctions
and
oil prices
or the lack of food for the hungry
and disease that preys on the many.
now,
maybe i'm too sensitive,
i've been called that in the past
but I am a believer in humanity
and if it don't
sound good
smell good
taste good
then it probably isn't.
the fight is the fight
there shall always be one,
only it is oneself
that we are fighting against.
believe it to be true
as I walk along these new york city streets
with
whites,
blacks,
browns,
reds,
yellows,
blues

it feels good,
almost like sunshine
wondering whether
to go for a smoke
or
stick with the drink.
my fight is my fight
still the same,
just on a different scope.
too much tragedy can bring any man down,
beware the buzzards
beware the vultures
the ones that loom overhead
silently skimming the sky
in the middle of an empty desert
sometimes
they know better.

girl friday

she
walked into
my life
from the streets of this fine city
like an angel from the darkness
a necklace across her neck read valerie
in gold glittering letters
with a curvy v and a punctuated e
but i,
i like to call her val
and val,
oh
she 's good
very good to me
and she 'll be good
to you
if you want her to,
if you ask nicely,
but
don't beg
just wait
for her to
come
to you
the gold at the end of the rainbow
that first sip
that happy ending.

life as it is

i've resigned myself
to the facts
and the truth is
love hurts
acceptance is pain
drowning is a shitty way to go
kissing is so beautiful
business is complicated
so are feelings and emotions
yet,
they don't have to be.
silence is golden
sharing is kindness
understanding is maturity
holding hands is bliss
like morning coffee and a cigarette,
after a night of lovemaking.
and then
the unexpected late night phone call
that you hoped would come,
gracing your mind like goose bumps
because
life is hard
these moments go by so quick
while memories become photographs
and
pretty soon the sun will set
another night shall approach
summer is near its end
and i'm tired.
i would
wish upon a star

but none are shining tonight
so
i just blow out a candle
and hope.
truth remains
the same
for those
that believe
and life
isn't the fairy tale i read about in books
life is hard
no matter who you are,
i realize
the human race is one
yet we resist to accept
and simplicity is everything
so is love.
and air conditioning is sublime
in this new york city heat.

it could of.

listening
for whispers
in a
crowded hallway.
looking
at the
many eyes
for a
second glance.
trying
to be hero
when
no one needs saving.
my fear
of success
outweighs
that
of failure
and still there is
hesitation
like a shadow
on an overcast day.
but
if i
knew you
for more than
these
 few passing seconds.
time.
could.
stand.
still.
but temptation

sits on the
ocean floor,
anchored unmoving
while
time
continues to
slip
away
just
as
baby's breath.

for those looking

Can't make sense
Of this town, its people
These very streets
This very room.
Becoming a vagabond of sorts
In the new world order
And it tears at owns' soul
Drape the mirrors
Pull the curtains
Shut the lights
I am not this
This is not me
Little by little
Everything is simply
Black and white
Plastic mannequin product
With a pink sugar coating for sweetness
But the colored flowers hold true
As they shall always
An awakening for those looking
An oasis for imagination
Can't make sense
Of much of anything
The hillside view
The overcast sky
Strength in just believing
Far outweighs our reality
Of what we are given.

57 degrees and rain

a city's lost its sight
all the angels fallen asleep
saints disappear through the fog and rain
and i am blind to see
all that there is.
buildings reverberate as echoes of secrets
and whispers
like the lies i tell
just like the great poets sit
rocking in their seats
cranking out words ideas thoughts emotion
plain beautiful descriptive shit
in the rain and thunder and cold
and there's only one light in a one souled room
coughing from contemptanguishangeralloftheabove.
stillness, i crave stillness
from that blurry double vision.
can't see much from the outside in
even with the blinders sitting on the floor
i wish i could blame it on the wine
blame it on the smoke
blame it on anybody but me.
but anything can happen on any day
not much though when there is no day
and all that is
isn't anything,
but a blue grey mass of fleeting passing air
and it's not moving.
the view from the window
is an old new york photograph
and it's not moving for now
neither am i
and neither is this poem.

untitled ii

and it breaks down to three simple
words
It's the way
we live our lives
and
here i find
myself
five to ten
while the night
settles itself
upon the day
alone & listless
pretending things could be
like they are in the movies
realizing they can't
yet still
here at the keys
searching in the early hours
for some thing
to settle the confusion
that sits
within me like a disease
i am a young soul
yearning
for the wisdom of an old soul
and
waiting
       waiting.

eastern daylight.

And there are sorrows
on the merchants eyes
stained leather boots
with burgundy smiles
this town feels cold
with smells of yesterday
and concrete wood and death and silence.
I called out your name tonight
hoping you would hear
but I was left with nothing,
which is something more than what I got.
dry wine
lonesome nights
broken down melodies ringing in my ears,
as the laughter of the mice
scurry through the walls.
so I turn on the radio
to tempt my thoughts
with the purity of classical moments
encrypted messages of love and hate
just as the poem in the bathroom stall.
static headaches
broken hearts
drunk from the drink at three a.m.
wagner never had it so good,
neither did the angels
but here we are, sitting pretty.
when the candles blow out
wait for the wishes to come true
the saints are living proof
that the absurdity of the ages
are simply whispers of a jealous soul.
there is a kindness in strangers
when you look into their eyes
and all our sadness
all our fears

the moaning cello
a dancing ballerina
and me
pass by
as the second hand
of a clock that used to
hang upon this rusty nail.
all that was
will be again.

drinks and conversation on a monday night

the night has a new meaning
when you are with a woman at a bar,
maybe it's the glance of her eyes
the way the candlelight shimmers
just the way she holds the glass
and smokes her skinny cigarette.
she plays with her napkin
and ruffles the corners
as i watch the way her hand moves.
delicate hands with long gentle fingers.
she's got good hands to hold
or so i think to myself.
cause the second round is on its way
and it's to soon
to say what i'm thinking.
the scent of perfume, her perfume,
drifts my way as a message of hope
which could be my salvation
but i'm still waiting for that next round
just as the night waits for day.
the young lovers that fill this bar
are hungry with anticipation
desperately seeking to fill the void of loneliness
but i been down that road and i think she has too,
when the quiet moments become your best friend
and all that seems to matter is simply that
which you have been trying to avoid.
her smile reminds me of a dream.
her skin like white sheets on winter mornings.
i been here before
when the words move freely

and the heart stirs as the ice melts away.
to curse these moments
would be a sin,
but so would reveling in them.
not here and not there
just caught somewhere in between
while all the meanings remain mysteries
yet she and i remain true
the same way we left before.

2 a.m. serenade

the kids next door
are going at it
again.
i can see 'em
through my window
cause
       they
left the windows wide open.
and lucky enough
he's got no curtains
so i sit
here in the dark
having a smoke
gazing upon drunken love,
i know this as she holds a beer bottle askew.
and lust and fondness and security and ideas
of
all the beauty
between   man
              and
                  woman
fall to the waist side.
but then my mind starts to wander again.
i'm halfway through the smoke
and the kids next door
are still going at it.
though for some reason they keep stopping
she puts up resistance
to his sloppy vodka and tonic advances.
he says whatever you say at 2 a.m.
she steadies
swigs off the michelob light
and goes in for more.

candlewax
drips
melts
a crescent moon
places itself over the night sky
shadows scatter as the bats fly overhead
and love finds a home.
just
like
that.
i put down the smoke
take a last taste
of some fine silver tequila
and go to bed.

And freedom

Finds itself
On rainy mornings
A faint voice
Of one I use to know

And hands
That once
Were held
Lay numb in scattered sunlight

And souls
Flutter amid
Four p.m. traffic
Yearning in seatbelts
While tears gently descend .

drunk impressions.

I have nothing more to say
Except these inner truths
That seem to be
The only reality that I have left.
I have fallen in love
But
It is with a woman
Who just might be the wrong one.
I sit in silent trepidation
Like some love stricken slave
Bearing the weight of the masses
Bearing the weight of ones own soul
And it hurts
Deeply
To see love as one imagined it to be
To see a soul as one thought it to be
To feel loss
As one has never felt,
And still I sit
In mere silence,
A dumb deaf mute
Pretending with smiles
As I drink from the glass of hemlock
Praying
It will be just one more swallow
And then I may rest,
Like all the romantics have,
The ones before
The ones to follow.

(suckers.)

I'm losing my train of thought

As the minutes tick by
But the feeling remains,
Like a sickness,
Love lost and punch drunk
The only reality I have left.
I have fallen in love
Only this time,
Love has not fallen for me.

bitch.

Ah,
the beauty of the red wine
takes its place on the stage
and i
sit here alone
again
like some fearful fearless soldier
in the black of midnight
stuck to watch the line
while the ants crawl
and the rain falls down
i am growing cold
towards you
and i feel it
like some drunken poison
that has no excuse,
as the clock strikes midnight
and the phone remains silent
just as
my lips
      your lips
      your heart
my heart
and the series
is even
at a game
a piece.

substance to the moments

      the maid
   hasn't yet
        arrived,
debutants
    and carnivores
wait in line
for the parade of fools
to leave room 422
And
      justification lacks
as does reasoning.
but there is
    substance to the moments.
Still.
And the boy
   that cried wolf
Isn't crying
 anymore.
   he is silent

as the wind
as sunlight
as the wisdom we share.

there are gypsies

on the streets of l.a.
scurrying up and down
cracked sidewalks
hopeless and forlorn
just as used old china dolls
in the antique shop on
Hollywood and Western.
And
the gypsies can pull you in
mesmerize
like
cherry red rock candy
like
a neon sign
flashing
on the sunset strip,
teasing,
enticing playfully
with the imagination.
this Disneyland
for the soulless & uninspired
a candyland board game for the masses.
And the whole world
is only 20 minutes away
no matter where you are
as long as
you do what you do
between the hours of 10 and 2.
And
the gypsies
will preach,
the gypsies
will pray
even make you a believer.

perfection for a september afternoon.

And it started
with a call for a new job,
            training starts next week.
decided to take walk in the park
        sweated
            day dreamed
        slept.
perfection for a september afternoon

 no clouds
sunshine
called a girl
  i been sleeping with
                    just to hear her voice
  (i'm simple like that).

3.30 pm
the drinking begins
   today
vodka and juice

4.30 pm
   the drinking continues
now
vodka and tomato.

i'm spending the time counting my
        dimes
            nickels
        and pennies

as the job doesn't begin till
  a week
from now, so.
 any change can buy
     a drink
a promise
        a little time.

7.30 pm
 red wine from last night
tastes even better
     the
second time around

and i suppose
     that is like love
but i haven't known
     that just yet.

and here it is
     half
past midnight
still going
     breathing
and striking the keys.
        not   bad,

not too bad

at all.

the days of wine and roses

there's a picture of on my wall
black and white
of apartment windows in paris.
the picture is crooked and beautiful.
a silent day in a silent city
with wooden shades open to the day
and paris
with all her years.
miller walked those streets
hemingway too,
those were the real ones,
the true rebels,
it's where miles played his horn round midnight
while parker stood off to the side,
jiving to the music,
sweet sweet music.
those were the days
in between here and there
and all the time in the world
to simply find out.
so i drink the red wine tonight
and salute the masters.
to the days of wine and roses,
rejoice in this bohemian rhapsody
these honest drunk moments
make it all worth it,
make me remember where it all comes from.
the time has come around again,
just as the winter days
for late night ballads
and poetry under the influence of it all,
that makes complete sense to me now
but not mean a thing in the morning.

the smoke hangs off my lips,
waiting to be lit one more time
the matchbook is from a bar downtown
some french joint in the meat district
where the whores and the hustlers
work the street corners,
the lonely ghosts of the night
and i pass them by
in a yellow taxi cab heading back uptown
to a room i consider home.
i pour what's left of the wine
into a fancy glass
and sip it slow.
another day has passed
a night lingers
but the song is coming to a close
so put out the candle
and let me sit in the silence
of this room
in the stillness of this night
with a black and white memory
of a paris afternoon
as the grey clouds passed overhead
and i,
drinking a coffee on the Champs Elysees
writing words on paper napkins
hoping for some wisdom to appear
while i'm not looking
but
all i can hear are the dump trucks
scurrying down the city streets
taking me from there to here, back again
yet i'll take anything at this point
any glimpse of truth or honesty
for just a moment
is worth everything.
and these memories are just that.

Only the foolish (fall in love)

Not even midnight
And my heart weighs
Like that of a storm
And i'm not afraid of death anymore
Learning to accept fate
Isn't as hard as it seems.
It is all acceptance,
And though it can be painful,
There is always much worse.
Only the foolish
Hide in the shadows.
Only the foolish
fall in love.
Only the foolish
reveal their fears.
Only the foolish
drink themselves into the night.
And here I stand
Swaying with the wind
Like a cork in the ocean
Drunk as those before me
And all those yet to come.
Maybe it is a disease
Or just loneliness gone mad,
Yet all this time
with so much to do
And still so few moments
To do it with.
I'm close to opening another bottle,
Though something within me
Says no.
But then again,
Only the foolish
Resist that temptation.
The eloquence of sarcasm
        On a cool autumn night.

Only the foolish (part 2)

Dream
Believe
Wish
Run
Hold hands
Write poetry
Kiss
Hug
Make love
And love in return
Read the newspaper
Smell flowers
Eat vegetarian only
Cheat
Hide
Listen
Watch commercials
Sit in silence
Watch sports
Drink beer
Wine
Tequila
Play jazz on vinyl records
Watch black and white foreign films in
     silence
          just to see
the beautiful images
Eat meat
Smoke
Dance
Fight
Curse

Say I love you just because
Desire
Travel
Laugh
Cry tears when without
Fall in love
Drive
Go to bed early
Do the 9 to 5 thing
Fuck
Do this
Read books
Watch cartoons
Look into another's eyes
                and see one's own soul
Romanticize
Light candles
Have children
Take bubble baths
Gaze at the stars on cold nights
fall in love
fall in love
fall in love
fall in love.
Only a fool.

Dried flowers.

I never understood the laws of physics
Neither
The laws of love,
But the company of strangers
And the company of you
Remind me of a dream that
One reads about in books
And to find it in this life
Feels as a dream
On november mornings
While the innocence of youth
Fades from me
Just as these words will one day
And tulips
Daisies
Sunflowers
Will continue to grow
Then continue to wilt
But something shall always remain.
Something
  Always
    Remains.

Malbec / 2000

Within me
An animal rests
A beast
Tied within a cage
Knowing
Possessing
The answers to escape this maze.
But still caught by compromise
By my own inadequacies
And to know that,
 is my own fault
And to be drunk before midnight
Is pure luck
Yet the rest is just stupidity
Twenty-seven and still figuring.
I saw purity today
In the form of a woman who passed by my way
For a just a moment
A faint glimpse
A faint smell of perfume
A smile and glance of the eyes.
I did not speak a word
Holding on to hope like a prayer
In this godless sanctuary,
Yet I still believe.
More than those who call themselves saints
More than all the priests combined
Patience is my religion
And I wait
In the silence of an empty room
For love
For understanding
For compassion
For truth, honesty
A hand to hold
And a place to rest my head.

scratching the walls

the world
can
be
 a pisser
            on rainy days
and
             hot steamy ones too

Love

         bites
     me
in the back
 li k e
           a
 bee
            s ting

and

 it HURTS like hellfire

       like
a
migraine

…but

it could be worse.

maybe,
         the glory days

are yet to come

cause

      they sure as shit
           haven't hit yet

at least,

i'm hoping .
          i'm hoping.

Sometimes
      that is all

    one

  can do.

silent whispers

And

the
silence
in
this
room
means
more to

me

than
any
words
that

you

could
ever say

Yet,
I
am
here

And
so shall
remain

For

Now.

And they say.

While the tube plays
I'll finish
What is left in the bottle
Pop a pill for the headache
And hope for a better tomorrow
Some say I should quit
But they are just
the non-believers
They are just
the excuse
for the repeats and repercussions
of the idle banter that keeps recycling in my head.
I hit the mute button
And the words flow
as if they were there
this whole time.
It would be better it I could type
Cause the ink is low
and
the lead gives you cancer, or
whatever the #2 gives you these days,
that's not
in the air,
in the food,
in the water,
in the drink that warms the liver.
And
And
They say exercise
They say don't drink soda
They say eat less meat.
Drive less

Love more
Work smarter
Not harder
Read more
Write more
And
They just might be right.

i will speak to you tomorrow.

If i could spend
        the

rest of these days

        typing at
the keys.

        i would be a happy man.

Yet i suppose

                i

would be happy

        If
i was getting laid
                        consistently

        Through the rest of these days
In the morning
                Noon
                        And night.

Making love

and

  Sometimes just
                A good
                        fuck.

Kissing with an
Open mouth

The feeling of a naked body
            against mine
                        melting within me.

and the warmth of skin touching skin

&

The heat

    And
                    Weight of another soul.

Like
        An iron vest

From the dentists' office.

And all I keep thinking about are

stars
        disco balls
    the swaying of leaves on oak trees

In the dusk of an October sky

And

        How I feel when I am with you.

Just like in the movies.

I smell the perfume
Of lost love
In the night time sky,
As it swirls and rests within me
As some lonesome friend
Whom I've never met
But have known before.
Just as silence
Just as friendship
Just as love
The broken truths we all live behind,
Pretending them to be real
When we are the melted wax
Of scented candles
Evaporating slowly into nothingness.
I have grown accustomed
To the quiet nights
The empty bed
The wine filled cups
Sweet beautiful serenades
Desperate tears that fall from my eyes
Soft breezes through my windows
Memories of kisses upon my neck and lips
And the feeling of a woman in my arms
Drink after drink
And no more smoke
Wanting a hand to hold
The scent of hair to caress my face
Noble words that no one will read.
Yet the candles still burn brightly
And the records continue to play
While all the beautiful sweet endings
To all the tragic stories

Find their way home,
Just like in the movies.
But still I wonder
Why.
How.
Have I sinned in this life
Or in one past.
Still attempting to make peace
With all that has gone wrong,
And on a road less traveled
There is always a final destination.

nothing really

sinful
     nights   at
    68   degrees
in the
     middle
 of november

and the taxi cabs
    climbing the avenues
m o v I n g
desolation
 from   street
         to street
remain empty

the kids have gone   home
except
  the band
drunken and stoned
and me
       waiting   by the way out

charlie
 is telling another story
      to the sad tune playing on stage
yet
the cats   keep smiling
cause   IT
      never sounded so good.

i'm
all out
of smokes
and conversation.
there
seems to be
NoTHiNG
to say anymore

but i guess

the silence &
broken melodies

of early morning yawning

is   something   to be   remembered

while the city lights that

shine as stars

dissolve
and
fade.

the trumpet player

of all the
glorious
things about this city,
to
simply
open the window
to the world
outside
can change the whole perspective.
everything
has new meaning.
everything
has its own story.
a black spotted cat
sits on a windowsill
in the apartment across
from me,
an unseen
trumpet player
plays a sad love song
and
it echoes and reverberates
in the alleyway below
as the sparrows sing a melody
and tires and sirens
float like a daydream
through these windows
and the sound
from his horn
feels like wind
and innocence,

all the joys of youth
that remain within
us
and
on a crisp
summers day
i was trying to see forever
but i realized
it didn't matter
cause i got right now
and that's all i need.

thanks to joseph campbell

rainy day
a saturday afternoon
found something good on tv,
a little bit of insight
for this world around us
cause that's what's been on my mind
lately.
and bill makes a comment
about
    what eden was
or rather
    what eden will be
and joseph
the cautious old man
with serenity at his finger tips
  quietly
        replies

  eden
   is.

and then
i knew
that
he knew.
this is what you have
this life
this is eternity
and i try
to grasp hold
of the circle of existence
but

it will never be possible
sometimes you get it
sometimes you don't
it is
the experience
it is
the journey
it is
all around.

it
is.

as the wise man says
'follow your bliss'.

a hollywood chorus

and as the sun sets
on this side of paradise
i'm back in hollywood
once again
back in the land of sunshine and lollipops
the eternal candyland and
oooh, it feels nice.
six months have passed
but everything stays the same.
with a few bucks in my pocket
we head into the pizza joint
for a pitcher and a pie.
and with nothing on my mind
except the cool taste of the beer
as it fills my empty stomach,
i am truly in a perfect place
and then it happens,
like out of some movie
she walks from the back room,
this slight little thing
couldn't have been older than 27,
dressed in her white button down shirt
black pants and a stained apron,
her hair tied up in a knot
and a smile that bleeds sex,
she approaches the table.
'i saw you before' she says
'is that so' i say
'yes, on my way here, on my way to work,
i saw you pass me'
she has beautiful eyes i think to myself.
'you have a good memory' i say.
she smiles that luscious smile

i sip my beer.
she tells her story
in between her tables
telling of her bastard boyfriend
telling of her shitty job
and how
she has to leave the country in two weeks
back to wherever it is that she comes from,
somewhere in europe,
maybe paris, maybe london,
it was the second pitcher.
and we let her talk her talk
content with the pizza, the beer
her conversation.
and as we make our way out the door,
you can tell by the look in her eye
she wants to come along.
'what time are you off'
i whisper under my breath
'12, maybe 12:30'
'well, maybe, we could...'
'give me your number' she says.
and the night begins,
but not until 2:30 a.m.
when the call finally comes
after the bars have all closed
and the city has shut down.
me and nick pull up to her place
it must be 3 by this time
and like an angel sent from the guy upstairs
she graces the lobby
her hair down,
wearing some see through leopard skin skirt.
damn it's good to be back, i think to myself.
'come in a second,
        my boyfriend wants to meet you'

....'what'....

'my ex wants to meet you'
i pause,
    thinking it all through
cause the pitchers turned to shots
and the shots turned to joints
and with blood shot eyes and a stagger in my step
i couldn't think of a reason to say no.
she looked so sweet
and i was so lonely.
and come to think of it,
it wasn't so bad,
he was a nice guy from paris
kinda short, little balding
a paparazzi photographer she says.
'well, it was nice to meet you' i say
and head out the door
me and nick
and this guys' girl.
3:30 a.m.
back at our place
we drink what's left of the tequila
sip some amaretto
and talk shit,
she makes a pass at me
follows me to the bathroom
telling me all i want to hear
it was me,
i was the one she saw on the street.
and now it starts to make sense
as she turns the lights off
and pulls me close
her mouth the taste of sour amaretto
and oooh, it feels good.
night turns to day
and she wants to go home.
what the fuck i think to myself.
'ok' i say.
i don't understand her way
this goddess of the night

yet i do what she wants,
anything,
as long as i can sleep as soon as it's over.
and as we pull up to her place
the ex pulls away.
'follow him, follow him'
i follow him to a red light,
she gets out the car
and stands like a child at his door
waiting to be let in.
the light turns green
and he drives off
leaving her standing alone.
god damn i think to myself.
she gets in my car
tears pouring
from those beautiful helpless eyes.
'take me to my hotel, but don't leave me'
she curses her ex,
she curses the night
and i drive silently on.
we walk to her room
on the second level
of some trashy motel suite
and there in front of her door,
her suitcase and two boxes.
'that fucking bastard' she says through tears.
'i should go'
'don't go, stay, please'
and i lay on her cheap motel bed
questioning the night,
questioning her ex,
this girl from a pizza stand,
questioning myself.
and she kisses me
and i kiss her back
and she cries in my arms

this poor gentle creature.
fucking hollywood, california.
shit like this must happen everyday
only tonight
it happened to me.
i left after a few hours of sleep,
leaving her undisturbed
under the covers.
and nothing happened that night
but everything happened,
all in a matter of a few hours.
i never saw her again,
didn't hear from her,
certainly didn't eat pizza again.
and that's the way it happens.
just like that
when you least expect.
shit happens,
sometimes good
sometimes bad
yet none the less,
shit just happens
and that's how it happens.

one last thing

i pray for
late night serenades
blissful moments
and drunken joy
at three a.m.
a light for my smoke,
a hand to hold
while i make my way home
on a summers night.
cigarettes and sweet perfume
gracing the air,
the smell of a woman.
the smell of her hair.
the smell of her skin
gracing the sheets,
lingering
as dew on morning flowers
and memories of childhood.
i pray for
moments like that.
those are the ones
that make all the sense,
order out of chaos
or something like that.
while somewhere
galaxies are forming
and stars are dying.
yet the sun begins to break
across the horizon,
as the night watch man
finishes his duties
and the garbage trucks
roll out of the avenues.
and
here i lie.

oh me

my only truth
are these words.
i am not like the rest,
a line divides
me and them.
and i can't tell
if they will understand
and i don't know
if they can understand
my simple thought
the struggle for words
my intentions at integrity.
i am one of many
a tiny piece
of it all
a man in a room
on a street
in a city
in a country
that is struggling to survive
in a world
that is struggling to survive
and i stand here
with open arms
a clear mind
a loving heart
curious
and patient
for insight into the way
of this world.
knowing a time shall come
when all will be one
and the meaning shall become
clear.

On a Sunday

i'm reverting back to all
my heroes,
the drunks
poets
nomads
still seeking solace in
the bottles of red wine
some bit of comfort
for the feint of heart.
to give up
on everything
at this point
seems of no use.
i have tried
i have
       followed
            all that i believe
i have tried
i have
            fallen in love
i have tried
       and
i have
       lost
i'm reverting back to someone
my heroes
    were not.
the drunks
poets
nomads
have all died
going down a road
i've never known

frightened beyond word
with everything to gain
and
        a heart
                to lose.
to give up
is not who i am

so
i try
    to follow what i believe
i try
    to love

And

still i am

still

i am.

from the morning

the lilacs of winter
shall always bloom
in spring,
while life and its many notions
dance in this morning sun
that seeks
to break through
a low grey sky.
i wish to play
as a child without
care or
        concern,
i remember
what innocence once was
and i am
so   f a r
from where i started
that i can only
keep going,
yet without the truth of innocence
but still a truth no less,
while the lilacs of winter
move freely
in the spacious sky
and open their hearts to love,
on a cold brisk morning in april,
as i remain still
holding on to a glimmer of hope
just cause i can.
knowing that
love
does exist,
always existed
and this love
too,
shall bloom in time.

rainy day & 54 degrees

and
        all
I
      think about
is
 you

the rain
              and
                      this

empty heart

to put
            these feelings   to words
is
      beyond me

just as
            these days

pass
                  me by
like
          the

winter moon.

twenty questions
 (for the first date)

0. what can i get you to drink?
1. where are you from?
2. and how was that?
3. how long have you lived here?
4. can i buy you another?
5. what's that scent you're wearing?
6. how was your day?
7. busy?
8. how is it working there?
9. do you want another round?
10. shall we grab a table?
11. would you like to share?
12. maybe,....a bottle of red?
13. what's your sign?
14. really? are we a match?
15. what are you having?
16. isn't that an aphrodisiac?
17. have you heard the new sade album?
18. why baby,
        do you look so damn good tonight?
19. what are you thinking?
20. shall we leave?

the cape

i stare at this blank white paper
while all the lovers have gone home
a sunday evening dissolves
 a w a y
and the night angels
carry us oFF
  t o   sleep
bringing dreams and visions
        of days to come,
colors of the rainbow
           melting from the sky
while another sad story
is printed on the page.
what is to become of us,
the loners and poets
vagabonds and whores,
all those looking for love
    and moments
for red wine and smoke
dreams and promises drifting through the air,
the endless summer,
and something to hold on to,
if not for just a few seconds.
and i'm drifting away
as the seconds tick by
losing track of time and space
and i'm drifting along
following where the road leads
where the rainbow ends
searching the ends of the earth
for truth and love
and meaning
yearning for good hope
peaceful tranquility
and a soft pillow to rest this heavy head.
we are all alone in this world.

june 5th

9:40 a.m.
a kid climbs
the brooklyn bridge
says he's got a bone to pick
with the state of our world
he climbs the high wire
till he reaches the top
but he won't let go.
this is what we have come to
this is what we have become
we are all trying to escape
we are flies
stuck against a clear glass window
buzzing buzzing buzzing
to find a way out
its right there
in front of us all
we are flies
stuck between a clear glass window
buzzing buzzing buzzing
but
we can't find the way
and they tell you to just
hold on
that is all you can do
stay sane
that is all you can do
don't jump
that is all you can do
they tell you things will get better
you are in a good place
luck, they call it
yet maybe
luck
might have just run out

yet no one knows.
and the kid atop
the brooklyn bridge
holds on
to the metal wire,
cuts in his hand,
smoking a cigarette
five hundred feet in the air,
sky above
the east river below
and death resting on his shoulders,
still negotiating with the cops
on the ground.
only two choices
on a partly cloudy day

stop
or
go.

and that's the best its gonna get
in this life
in his life
but on the bright side of things
i heard some new music today
which is like
a food that's never been tasted
fresh, new and surprising.
while the sun shines,
it's a comfortable
74 degrees,
as the rest of the world
just
plays in the park

so
you never know.

Love. (part one)

like a cramp in the night,
that feels like a sharp knife.
like back pain
migraine headaches
sunburn
poison ivy
paper cuts
and rug burns.
like when you bite your tongue,
broken glass and bare feet
rainy days,
wet kisses,
holding hands
the scent of her skin
 at the base of her neck
the scent of her hair
tickling your face.
a warm body.
morning kisses.
the paper and a cup of coffee.
and
I beg for more
anything but the silence of this room
my empty words
spoken to strangers
I am without, always have been
while love sits with me
as a flower
simply waiting for the right time
to bloom.

when the morning comes

i hope to be here
when the sun rises
when the hangover settles
and life can be
just as i imagined it
could.
i come from
a desolate place
where land and sky meet
as one.
and solitude
is the only way
out.
it has rained for days
my clothes soaked through,
so i sit
by firelight
to warm what's left.
a sluggish yellow moon
attempts to be seen
in this black night,
a beacon of hope
for those
that continue to wander,
as i have.
luck
is for those that gamble
i leave it all to chance
and for that
one must have
simple will.

i dream
of a time
when all things shall
fall into place,
when there is sense
to meaning,
when the walls
that keep us apart
will disappear.

A l m o s t .

i woke up early this morning
and saw the sky was blue,
the breeze feels like fall
summer is coming to a close

a night in the life

as
softness
is
to a
lotus leaf
as purity
is
to a virgin
this place
was
none of that.
yet
we are all

SedUceD

by the smell
by the idea
by the pretty people
descending
upon
the underground
nightlife
in all it's
rancor and glory.
velvet rope
and
attitude
in waif like skin
pompous heirs
and gold rolexes.

while the hum
of the city
reverberates within you
like the days
in harlem
years ago,
but this ain't that

sEDuCeD

by seduction
just like
a first kiss,
as love
to
young lovers,
so this could be
but
just
isn't.

bessie's lament

and bessie
asks for a cup of coffee
from outside the restaurant doors
three sugars and some milk.
with only her
  self
natty dreads and
  a big blue smile
that gots
         no teeth.
cause bessie seen the blues
tired from all the years
with a voice as deep as
garrison's bass
at three a.m.
she has a tale
though told not by an idiot,
she seen noah and jesus
drank wine with elijah
made love to moses
she seen wars
blood and death
she tasted famine,
disease.
bessie seen the blues
she sang of the blues
on open mountaintops
wept under the willow trees
mourned all those that came before
and didn't make it.
and bessie
sips her coffee
with three sugars and milk

as a queen she once was
and will be again
cause bessie seen the blues
but she seen
the yellows,
reds,
greens,
oranges,
and
purples too,
she seen them all,
such is the way
when angels are amongst us.

the big IF on a sunday afternoon

I decide on a beer
As a way to pass the late night hours
Cause the pills stopped working
But my mind keeps going over
And over the same things that
I'm drinking and pilling
To get away from.
I'm talking of love
And it's many discourses.
The moments on rainy nights
The ones on cool evenings
Afternoons
Early mornings and then some.
I've tasted love with these lips,
Held it in my arms
while the sun descended
from the horizon.
I've smelled her skin
And it reminds me of a summer sky
I pretend that my simple moments
Could be lifetimes.
The truth remains as I thought it would be
So many times before,
As love remains a tulip
blossoming in spring.
I am and shall always be
Just as these thoughts feelings emotions
And she remains
As she was before,
Not mine, not theirs,
Just something wonderful
Like you see in a black & white movie.
And oh,
        I want this life to be just like that,
Happy endings and everything.

late monday night

it isn't gonna work
not at this time
certainly
yet the mayor agrees
and so does the city council
but here i sit
a little after twelve a.m.
waiting for the pills to start working,
hoping something will appear across
this page as reason to go on,
cause lately,
the well has been dry
these pages remain blank
and still so much resides within me,
more than i could ever express in words
phrases metaphors hyperboles
and the rest of the shit they taught in school.
yet all my heroes reside in books
authors musicians beggars
drunks and gamblers.
so fuck you
and
the horse you rode in on.
you tell me you know the truth
and the truth is filled with nothing
but lies
because
then i say that cursed word
i meant it from every inch of my soul
yet here i remain
not with you, though
longing for you as heartache

as sunshine
as breathe
as life
there is a whole world out there,
which I want nothing to deal with,
not tonight
not with my single steps
i know what lies out there
and i know what lies within
that
which is pure
which is me.
which you know not of.

midnight on 42nd street

ten years ago
this was a different place.
ten years ago
we were different people.
but the neon lights shine
same as they did back then
only now,
the pimps and whores
have moved downtown
to the meat packing district
which is fitting
in a peculiar way.
the druggies
the alkies
they're still here,
hiding in the shadows
fixed on their fix
and the homeless
still roam this street
just to find a solitary spot
warm enough to keep them alive through the night.
i wrap myself in this torn winter coat
fighting the cold wind,
struggling through the crowds
heading to 8th avenue
passing filled bars
with empty people
and empty conversations,
loneliness in its' purest form.
i think about heading in,
having a drink

but i'm out of cash
and out of luck,
such is the way on 42nd street.
life is what it is,
with all the desperation
that lingers as sickness on the street corners,
there is a way out of it all,
i think,
with all the lost love that hides itself
in the dim apartments.
simple people
searching and yearning
for simple things,
yet in this crowded city
you can get so consumed
and lose sight of it all.
such is the way on 42nd street
and all the other streets,
alleys,
and avenues.
such is the way in this beautiful city,
new york city.
so i descend into the underground
take the local c train uptown
numb from the cold,
lost in my own world,
immune to it all.

wisdom lies in madness

I am left with no choice
But to throw away all the principles
That they have taught,
All the lessons learned.
For I
Am not like the rest
The fools
The masses
Those caught in the drudgery of
Nine to five.
Stuck in the corner of this
White walled room
Drowsiness
And hunger
Fill me to the core.
And still I sit
Contemplating knowledge
That lies within my reach,
Yet still I am too far away
To touch
To hold
To grasp
That wisdom lies in madness.
And all the beggars
Must know all that I don't
Just as my elders
Who stand beside me
Know,
All that I do not.
While the booze
Poetry
Books

Quiet
Tear me apart
From the inside
And this lonesome soul
With everything to give
Shuts the door
To the outside world
And all I am
Is
All I am.

the first round

and like a warrior
in the field of battle
the boxer steps in the ring
it's a three to one shot
a young fella
from up there in harlem
with eyes of lucifer
and the courage of zues.
he is the lion
that roams open savannah
methodically calculating
each step
awaiting the kill
soon to take place.
the bell rings
echoing like thunder
between city walls.
the lion prances
gliding easing
focusing
ready.
one two punch to the left
    uppercut
    uppercut
jabjabjabjabjabjabjab
resist
hold back
watch him stagger
watch him flounder
now
a fake
straight to the gut

and then
a lightning right blow in the face

s tagg ger

st a gg er

st a ggg e r

hold back

resist
watch him
watch the fear in his eyes
balancing left right left
perspiration becomes blood
and he
   falls
as a star from space
rain from heaven
an angel on earth.

all bets are now
  OFF.

in the mood

it was a saturday night
there was nothing to do
the yanks are up by 3
it's the bottom of the ninth
the kids have turned in
while the rain falls
shattering the silence
and symphonies
of boyhood dreams.
but no use thinking about what's past.
the drink is getting cold,
my smoke is dwindling
crazier things have happened
only not usually on saturday nights,
like the one i got here
and it's too hot to go outside
too hot to even move
but if i move the chair just right
i can be in the cross hairs
of the cool blue jet stream
of air conditioned air,
so cold it makes my nipples hard
like moonbeams and lollipops
and kissing on the first date.
i popped open a beer
turned on the tube
rolled up another one.

when hunger falls silent

i sit at the door
waiting
while the sun shines on my back
burning inside outside
heating up like tar
like black pavement
90 degrees
that feels like 110
and there is no place to go to
no place for consoling the weak
the poor,
you or i.

i sit by the door
listening
as the smoke that rests on my lips
falls silent.
i fall silent,
not because i want to
but just because i have to.
these days aren't what they were
nor should they be,
but insistence rings
within like some monotonous tone
it ticks pops
twitches
jerks and pulls at me

and i sit at the door
thinking
it is hunger
that provokes the leopard
survival that quenches its thirst

poised for a kill
with tranquil patience.

and when hunger falls silent

the blue sky turns to black
shadows turn to night
and stillness becomes a friend.
there,
you will find me.

Love (part 2)

Love is at my fingertips
Waiting to escape
Yearning to define a word
That has no meaning,
while the hours tick by
And still I am left without you
A prisoner of sport
Of one's own shame.
Like silent kisses in the night
Placed upon a pillow
As I seek to explain
Mere emotion,
Drunk on words and wine
The essence of nobility for a mortal
Such as I,
And still love remains at bay...
Love as laughter
Love as tenderness
Love like red wine on a Wednesday night
Love as kindness
Love as you in my arms
While your tears run down your face
And you tell me of the silence you feel
When we are apart
Yet still I remain helpless,
Handicap to your rescue
As a thief in the night.
I know all the answers,
But not all the questions
As a distraught child lost
While my tears run down my face

And silence is restless
When I am not with you.
Yet you will never know
You will never know.
Love is a broken record
Love is my hand in yours
Love is our silence
Love is my body wrapped in yours
Love is a kiss upon your lips
Love is

silent.

i am
a
drum
    roll

when
i

b a n g

my
 head
against

the

WALLS

this
 f ea r
cuts

mE

to
 t he

c o re.

i
neeed
nnneeed

neeeed
 need.

i
need

like
    you   need.

but
give

         ME

first.

This is Unfinished.

i'm caught in a crossfire
of disillusion
where promises
are lies
and confusion is sanity.
this place is a river
of currents,
a whirlpool of indulgence
and self-pity is a slogan.
truth is blasphemy
with the volume turned up.
and you may shut the door
but it won't lock
you can close your eyes
but you will always hear
the silence.
and
the silence is deafening.
i once saw
an old man
drive himself into a wall
cause he lost consciousness
at the wheel
and his wife was
  screaming and pleading
as he drifted away
mind and body
sifted on wax paper, and
all i remember
is the silence.
the disparity of emotion
my own helplessness.

one last one.

the smoke rests upon my lips
matches in my hand
but i don't light up just yet,
i wait
for the right moment
the right words,
the right fucking anything at this point
just something.
these attempts at profoundness
Has become my medicine,
a nagging in the back of the neck
a twitch
and then it happens
like those sad ballads on rainy days
that just feel so perfect.
my fingers move without thought.
the days have been strange
nothing like i've seen
but i've felt this feeling before.
this feeling,
almost lost
almost death,
almost something out of reach
almost love
almost perfection
almost a beautiful day
almost something.

i light the cigarette
and the smoke feels good,
i'm quitting after this one,
definitely after this one.

this one last one.

all in the eyes

i am a child
with bigger hands
and bigger feet

a child,
grown up
and filled with curiosity

i am a child
in the body of a man
with a soul unborn

a child,
with longing eyes
and innocence

i am a child
yet wise as an old man
and still unsure

a child,
shy as a morning flower
before the sunrise

i am a child
with open hands
willing for a chance

a child,
with years of experience
and still knowing nothing

i am a child
yearning to love
and cautious of hurt

a child,
roaming unpaved streets
searching for a friend

i am a child
born into a life
i have yet to understand.

the promise of youth

the promise of youth
fades away
while night approaches
and rain continues to fall.
these years are catching up,
much to my surprise,
and expectations
become a curious thing.
answers and questions
become one in the same
and to survive is the only responsibility
one has to oneself.
if it ends up like it does
in the movies,
then consider yourself lucky.
the promise of youth
is a riddle
taught in second grade
it stays with us
and we hold on to
the ideals
the essence
the simplicity
yet it easily escapes our grasp.
so here we are
realizing there is nothing to hold on to
but the moment
precious seconds
minutes hours days.
the promise of youth
is a dream

but it does exist
maybe did exist
just as love
friendship
anger
jealousy
longing
and loneliness.

lucky

i'm lucky enough the safe flight
lucky enough for the shoes on my feet
lucky enough for a smoke at midnight
lucky that it's not cold right now
lucky to be here.
lucky enough to have lived and live
in new york city.
lucky enough for those mornings.
lucky to see
even though
there is so much bullshit out there
that it's hard to make any sense of it.
lucky enough to know.
lucky enough to not trust the experts
or the politicians
lawyers
evangelists and
hollywood.
lucky enough that the t.v. is broke
and the radio still works.
lucky enough for the red wine.
lucky enough to still dream.
lucky enough for afternoon naps
sleep at night
her warm body next to me.
lucky enough that she stayed for coffee
lucky enough
to have watched her get dressed
which was more beautiful than i
would have ever imagined.
lucky enough
for the paper delivered to my door.
lucky enough to have no pets.

lucky enough to have heard
miles
and
coltrane
ellington
and
nina
brubeck
chet and
louie armstrong.
lucky enough
to have bukowski on my side
or so i'd like to think.
lucky enough
for hem
the bullfights in spain
and miller in paris.
and lucky when he came back to ny.
lucky enough
to have tried to love.
lucky enough
to have felt it in return.
lucky enough
to have folks that i call my friends.
lucky enough
to remember.
lucky enough
for belief
and that
it's not what you think.
lucky enough
for a bed tonight.
lucky enough
to have looked upon the night sky
to have seen glistening stars
and smelled ocean air.

lucky enough
the weather calls for sun tomorrow.
lucky enough
to smile.
lucky enough
to be here
and
not there.
just lucky enough for this.

lullaby at 53'

defeat
rears it's head'
like some
lecherous tumor
and
i,
mere mortal
with only
simple hands
simple mind
waited for a sign
on the other end
that told me to
keep going
            keep going
so i
proceeded
with blinded eye
and
torn shoes
(the nobility of a king
on a sunday afternoon)
while
all the tulips & daisies
that parade across dreams
begin to fade
and wilt away
i spoke to you
in wordless whispers
begging upon the dawn
with unsatiated hunger

as the clock ticks
                    ticks
past present future
all at 4:24 a.m.
you're voice,
an echo
in my imagination.
falling light as rain
and i
in the dark
gazing out a seventh story window
charmed and lonely
with nothing to regret.
so
goodnight and
                    good morning
to you
drunks,
buzzards,
druggies and whores,
doctors,
acrobats,
the garbage men
and newspaper boys.
let the candles burn out,

shooting stars

i'm waiting for shooting stars
ready to make a wish upon the night,
sitting on this lonely mountain top
waiting for something to happen.
and it's not so bad to be here
in the cool autumn night,
it'll be put in the memory box, this one.
if my words could dance on the page ,
then they would dance to the music
that always plays in my head,
ain't no one around to take that away.
and if they could only understand
where i'm coming from
but even i question
where i'm coming from.
always questions,
seldom answers
in this estranged world.
and i'm looking for words to fill the page
but i can't think of a thing,
only that the tune sounds real good,
and i want to make love to a woman.
not much to ask of the night, is it.
but i'll settle for the rest of the page
and some good dreams
that should be enough for now.
the lights of the empire have gone out
and the rest shall follow.
so here i sit
waiting for my light to go out
waiting for the moon to guide me
waiting for my eyes to close
and shooting stars to fall.

stirred, not shaken

and
the vision of the african sunsets
dissipates in the wind
while the hope
        that lasts all of time
fills my cup
                spilling over the edge
staining the white tablecloth
nothing can help that which
            collapses
        when the gravity
    of all the fallen angels
        catches up to us.
still
what can be said
    of those feelings that hide within
resting   matriculating   becoming
        more and more real
i sense something to come
            and
        i am frightened,
                    of the truth
    in humans
when intentions speak louder than these
            attempts.
    my ideas of what i thought i would be
            are exactly
            what i am.

    but you,
        you
are not what i thought

certainly
not what was expected
 in this lifetime
more tangible than experience teaches
something
good
better than chocolate
   satisfying a heart that has longed
to be loved.

the kindness in flowers

And

 the tragedy
   of all errors
exists
 just as   the
          cancer in the smoke
and still
I
  wait like a fool
warming in morning sun
smoking a smoke
               sipping the potion
the
  heat feels of love
          as I would imagine it to be

and the kindness in flowers

is the   purity of rain.
    there   is
 sense to you
and
       t he
               way   I

feel.

Just as
   summer   &
     spring
  Winter
       fall

while
         steam pipes
               scream

and bus stops
                stay empty

my coffee

         gets
               cold.

a sonnet in b minor

and what more can i say
while the red bordeaux
inches its way to my head
as i've walked these streets like every man
and still
i sleep in an empty bed
yet the drunkenness eases the tension
her questions at the bar eased the tension
the look in her eye
her way
brought something to the monotony of friday nights
and i suppose that is all that one should hope for
in these early morning hours
cause in the end we are all alone
it's those precious moments we share
that means something
those are the times we are most alive,
the rest is merely anticipation.
but still i wait
for her to turn the corner
and join my parade.
i have an empty chair
a full bottle
and a story of what was
and what is
to share to one who will listen.
isn't much to ask the night
in the few hours before dawn,
it's all i got left
my special gift to give.
these nights are young
and i am getting old
yet the candle still burns

and a neon moon drifts by my window
reminding me of bullfights and roses
red wine in paris,
reading books in the park,
innocent days and sunsets,
those that came before
and those that are yet to come.
so i close the shades
my eyes and
rest this weary head.

conversations late one night

in this late hour
the song remains the same
just as the view from this window
i roll up some smoke
to complement the way i'm feeling
and little do they know
that it's all about the way you light it
and that will determine the rest of the journey,
till we get to the end
and the phone rings
it's a friend from l.a.
he tells me of the trip to vegas
and the drugs, the smoke, the girls,
salvation for the masses.
he had a good time.
he can't remember a thing.
he's down two grand.
damn, i wish i was there.
vegas in all her glory,
she's a pink cadillac and a pack of lucky strikes.
she's the single woman on the street corner
with a thumb in the air.
she's a roll of the dice.
do not forget
in the land of plenty,
there are always those without.
glitter and gold, he says
glitter and gold.
and
i think to myself,
the best part about vegas
is the drive away.

e / b / m

i held her hand
and anticipated her breath
felt the rain wash in my mouth
as i kissed her neck
while white lightning
ricochets off a sleeping city
thunder rolls beneath me
that feeling comes back again
like salt and chocolate
    jack and coke
    lemon and lime
like eloquence
and beautiful moments
that's the way it was
and to get this far
to recognize
whatever that feeling is
to know that it's still possible
even through these
days and nights
makes it all worth it
such is the way
with these futile attempts
at poetic verse
cause the other
is a hard thing to find
8 million stories in the city
and here i am
and here she is

and her hand
feels
 right
in
 mine
her
 breath
feels
right
against
my
skin
and the rain feels good
         as it washes our sins away

the mayor of 72nd street

stands tall
in the dusk of evening
it's been some time since the last time
he steps from side
to side
drunk with nobility
and drunk from cheap vodka
in small plastic bottles
he don't ask for much
just a little talk
maybe a joke
he talks in a soft slurred manner
on reflections of the days gone by
all that was
all that will be
and any spare change
for the flophouse tonight.
and that's the way it goes
for the saints in hiding,
the ones you don't see
or maybe you do
out of the corner of your eye,
who's to know these days
but the mayor
tells me things are good
the shack isn't that bad,
some place north of harlem
there's a new job that fills the spare time
and a woman that passes by
in the late afternoons
just to check up on him
a fine woman,

a
    fine
        woman,
cause the h.i.v. hasn't been a problem
but he hasn't been feeling the same lately
could be the winter days
could be.....any thing.
it's 6:58 p.m. and
neither of us says a word.
the streetlight flickers on
a bus drives by
hissing along the way
sirens scream from a distant avenue
and i feel the cold air
seep through my clothes
wish i was in l.a. right now,
and the mayor says
he'll be here till 9 tonight
i hope to catch you on the way back i say
and shake this man's hand
pass 'em a few bucks
depart into the night
and
hope to see the mayor before
        9
comes round.

america

the truth is
that we are all looking for a place
to call home.
and as the sun sets over the pacific ocean
on a thursday afternoon,
i can hear her faintly whisper
the words to the song playing over the radio
and i know what she is saying
as we drive along the pacific coast highway
toward nowhere,
and that is exactly the point.
a full moon stretches itself
across the darkening sky,
and i close my eyes
wishing upon the night,
wishing upon the first star i see.
i'm twenty-five
with a few bills in my pocket
some smoke to roll
and a woman driving this car
that could be the one,
but i'll never know-
at least not now, anyway.
but she feels good next to me
and that's all i need for now.
sometimes the anticipation is everything.
we ate at a place with a simple name
but you didn't pronounce it like that,
but the view was breathtaking,
she was breathtaking

and looking into her eyes
and she looking into mine
was everything for a moment in time.
but moments pass
just as the days
the hours,
the minutes
and it all becomes memories
in the end.
if only i could make them last.

searching for the right words for this one moment

and it isn't even close to midnight
yet here i am, back again so soon
the drink was good to me this evening
as i stagger to make sense of it all.
there is a full moon tonight
the empire state is purple
and i am drunk.
it must have been the margaritas on the empty stomach,
what else is one to do with the full moon fever
rising inside like jealousy,
except wallow in my pride
and everything else that lies beneath my feet.
i spoke to a woman over the phone tonight
didn't have much to say
yet we talked for a while bout nothing
but sometimes nothing means everything
and everything will do on a night like tonight.
cause this one will pass just like the rest
but this time i sit hunched over the keyboard
desperately
searching for the right words for this one moment.
it makes me laugh,
cause i keep doing this,
i keep coming back to these keys
for insight for wisdom for who knows what
but i'm glad i do,
if nothing else but to satisfy my hunger.
this is my poetry
these are my chronicles
these words, my life
everything i am at this point.
does it add up....
does it matter....
and my mind draws a blank
so let me go for now.

a friday morning

i thought
and therefore made my first mistake
as the gentleness of fallen leaves
stirs with innocence
and the grey december mornings
fade away to words on a page.
as to the nature of man
and the workings of the mind
no one can know that which is hidden
but if given a chance
anything can happen, almost like luck.
i keep thinking and
that shall be my demise in the end.
to escape you would be a lie
to hold you would be just.
still, loneliness rests her head upon the pillow
and i wake to a new morning
with her on my mind
yet again,
i can only beg on the charity of neighbors
as some sort of beacon of guidance
for this is nothing i have ever known
these moments,
like a dream to hold on to
while we sift through all that remains
just so that i can find you in a crowded room

home.

just one more sip
and i'll know where to begin
and it won't be politics
because fuck politics
and it won't be religion
because it's already been written.
with a few drinks in me,
who knows where to begin
while the box of cigars are empty
and the smoke all smoked
i sit absentmindedly
immune to it all
as the encyclopedia's rest on the shelf
the yearbooks remain dusted
and my memories are yellowed paper
taped to the wall
these are the days of old
a time that once was
yet isn't anymore
but the pictures still hang on the wall
the paintings on the ceiling fan
and the dresser and the door
the same old room
but looking with different eyes
an older soul.
this is where i'm from
this is the place
they call home,
yet this time
i feel like a visitor.

the kerouacian dream

woke up with nothingness
over my shoulders
and mediocrity on the empty pillow
next to me,
another morning
another day
i feel like a beat up fighter
hit too hard too many times
and still here i am
grinding away at this battle of evermore.
i have questions
but all my answers are contradictions,
there is no end to my persistence,
the nagging itch in the back of my head
telling me to keep moving ,
don't stay still.
stillness is peace and death.
and love,
what about it.
love is a cold shower on a hot day
love is a clean pair of underwear
love is being drunk on red wine
love is a moment that passes by so quickly you forget
love is just a word
and
words are my salvation
in this search for the kerouacian dream.
i been breathing this dusty air for too long
and it's killing me.
there must be somewhere else
anywhere but here,
just something more than this,
i don't know what,
maybe i'll know when i get there,
and then again,
maybe i won't

four things to remember on a night like tonight

i feel like crying in your arms
on this cold dark night
for no other reason than to be close to you.
my seclusion, i cannot explain
as i know nothing else
but these blues,
these depressing, invigorating, sad blues.
and if the words i write
are just regurgitations
of all the other attempts,
do they still count for anything?
      does this struggle for sincerity hold up to your
      standards,
whatever they be.
at summer's end,
the cool breezes float through the autumn night
and i am alone,
while the hands of the clock keep ticking
the record skips,
and the daydream ends.
so maybe she'll call
maybe she won't
but tonight, i think i'll stay right here.
close to the only things i know,
the red wine
the record player
the paper and pen.

all that falls between

the day calls for sunshine
yet it rains
as it does in london
this time of year,
but i take it all in stride
cause i got the city out this window
which is more than the others got.
i'll settle for the winter days
the winter nights
and all that falls between.
but it isn't much
to carry one through
with lost poetry
and sober mornings
to kill the time.
and the bed
remains empty
the toothbrush left alone on the toothbrush stand
perfume long gone
whispers turned to silence
but the creaking pipes
sirens
honking horns
people, oh the people
fill the empty space
of my mind
like a god damn headache
that no aspirin
can take away.

memories of you.

the sun begins its descent
in this far off place,
thirty three thousand feet in the air,
and all that i'm left with is her faint sweet smell.
it lingers on my lips,
like the words i wanted to say but didn't,
and it all seems like a dream as i knew it would.
i keep the window shades down,
so i can't look back,
my eyes closed,
so as not to see what stands before me.
the nights are restless in this cold city
and all i have sits in a bag by the door,
waiting for the word to get me out of here.

leaving is always the hardest part.

and to know you are there
eases the impatience of the hours,
yet, to know i am here
in a silent space
staring into a sea of grey
with this hunger, this growing hunger,
my hands empty
my heart full
i look on the twilight sky for inspiration
waiting for a star to shine in on this dark room.
and if i give it enough time,
it will.

closing time inspiration

i want to write something
but i don't know exactly what to say
i could talk about love,
or the absence of it
i could talk about this moment
sitting by my open window
looking out on new york city
in all its morning glory,
i could talk about the cold coffee
the unsmoked smoke,
(i seem to do that a lot)
i can reminisce
maybe think of the days to come
i could listen to track twelve,
'closing time' - tom waits
again and again
until whatever i'm feeling inside
escapes me.
i could do anything , i suppose
yet here i stay
struggling to get this something,
whatever it might be,
on the page before the song ends.
and
It's over already.

a night in november

the time says 9.06
eastern standard time
and i drank a bottle of wine tonight
some french wine
and it was good and now
i'm drunk
but sobering up as the minutes fly by.
and for the first time tonight,
i'm listening to the poems of Bukowski
some record of spoken word
and as he stumbles on the word
absurdity
i grin to myself
in my own little world
happy to be with him again.
there are certain things in this world
that make complete sense
like the sunsets
like love
like Bukowski on a november night
like red wine on a cold evening
like scented candles
like a phone call from a friend
like the bottle of tequila that
sits by my side.
yet somehow,
i am missing them all,
except the red wine and the bottle of tequila.
i'm missing the vocabulary
 for the things i want to say
and i'm missing.

i'm missing love in this dark hour,
i'm missing a friend
who's far away
yet so close in my heart.
i pause
and take a swig from the tequila
before i begin again.
so
so what more can i say
that all the others haven't
what can one do
oh,
what
can
one
do.

we all fall down

on a clear blue morning

just after dawn

i saw the sky falling

and the buildings

collapsing in

over and over

upon themselves

this is hell undone

this is a nightmare

this is worse than worse

and the screams of forgiveness

and the cries for help

have become nothing but whispers

and the disparity

rains over our heads

while peace and love,

the absurdity of it all

has become four letter words

silently cursed

under our breaths

yearning for prayers to be heard

as the walls come crashing down

our times will be changed

from this moment on

everything you know

is not as it appears

in these thick clouds of nothingness

we look for truth to prevail

yet truth is opinion

they are words that remain unspoken

just like the love lost

and dreams that have been washed

down the drain.

these tears are for those

i don't know

these tears are for what

i thought could be

these tears are for the

emptiness that sinks in my soul.

and this clear blue morning

has become a dusty sky

i was looking out my window

hoping to see forever

but it was no longer there.

american standard   (#23)

don't own a ford
but i take my coffee
with milk and sugar
and drink it quick
for the vitality in it's murky waters
and i smoke my smoke
without a conscience
because i'm off the drugs
except for television and
the five o'clock beer.
yet the mornings
arrive gently,
for the most part,
as i shake the weary night away
to once again enter
the bloodstream of life
with reluctance over my shoulders
and no clean clothes,
but good shoes
and that makes all the difference.
roaming the streets, the parks
traveling as if lead by a teacher,
in search of the american standard
and the sun feels nice on my skin.
the roads are crowded.
the sidewalks are lonely.
where is everyone going
i mutter
speaking to the sky
what are they searching for
i whisper

asking myself the same question
and the sign blinks don't walk
so
i walk faster.
the taxicabs fly like time
and time is bird
in search of prey.
and i struggle through the struggling
just to stand on my own two feet

before
        the
            sun
                sets.

and the night
arrives like a yawn
my arms stretching for shelter
reaching for the bar stool,
taking a seat,
watching the foam settle.
lost in the pleasures of a closing day.
the night sounds erupt like laughter
and the booze is comforting,
an only child finding a friend,
but still
i am not satisfied
incomplete
sifting through this life for decency
while the outside world beckons
to share in it's loneliness.
so
   i
    run.

i run from loneliness
               from exaggeration-
away from the standards
i've been told to follow

to find myself

alone in a room
with a pen and paper
a cold cup of coffee
and
still no ford.

american standard (#24)

i want to live like a king
but for now,
i'll settle with what i got-
this car
this road
a cup of coffee
and a full tank of gas.
i'm still searching
one year later.
redefined.
and redefining (the american standard)
yet,
as the day rises and comes to a close
is it this man and woman
in this semi-truck from oklahoma
this man riding his tractor
the woman hanging her clothes to the clothesline
the children playing ball in the street
the family in the mini-van
on the way to disneyland
the hitchhiker on the side of the road
the gas station attendants
the fast food manager
hotel clerk
police officer
what is their standard.
t.v.
cable
porn
art

literature
music
guitars and cigarettes
    on saturday nights
cowboy hats
and woman in convertibles
searching these roads
these small towns,
is it the loneliness.
can i get there from here.
or is it
love.
love is all there is.
love makes it all happen.

american standard   (#25)

sitting on this greyhound bus
headed for the big city
leaving this life
for a life i left behind.
i'm gathering the old stones
putting the pieces back together
to see what i got left.
passing through these small towns,
driving down main street
and no one is a stranger but me,
and i like it like that.
american flags
swing from gracious white porches
in this suburban dream.
and windmills and pick up trucks
tractors and baseball caps.
life is simple if you want it to be.
while the fields of wildflowers
move gently against the wind
i think of love and beauty
and not going back to that city.
i think of Kerouac and Hemingway.
i think of Bukowski and Miller.
and maybe i could just stay on this bus,
till the end of the road.
stay in motion until there is nothing left,
but there's always something left in the end.
the mountains have turned into buildings
this old country road is a highway

and the pulse of new york
rises like heat off the sidewalk.
but my mind keeps wandering
thinking back to the road,
a lonely stretch of highway
in the middle of nowhere
with nothing but sky and earth as friendship
and silence as thought.
it's a beautiful fucking thing,
and i miss it dearly.
Dylan plays over in my head,
such sweet eloquence,
he reminds me of the road too.
the greyhound isn't moving
cause the traffic is a bitch,
so, welcome home.
the bus rolls into the station
gate 29,
i pack up my things,
newspaper, coffee cup, a stick of gum,
my truth and my pride
and put it all in a bag.
stepping off the bus into the bright sunlight,
i think of the last line of 'the outsiders.'
sort of feels like that in a way.
the end to another chapter
and maybe
a story to share.

american standard (#26)

and in these hands
i hold on to all that remains,
love with its discourses
and the headache of all sorrows
evaporates into thin air
just as the smoke leaves my lips.
they told me to believe
and i did.
while the rain falls away
as the day breaks from
the ends of the earth
and sanity
was thrown a long time ago.
justification is useless
for us lonely strangers
yet the bed is still warm
from where you slept
last night.
the standards are
and shall remain
just what they are.
with a cup of black coffee
my smoke
a good pair of blue jeans
and used leather shoes.
my rattled mind
relaxes in its shell
while the quest for truth
falls from outside to
within.
the lizard king,
in all his glory,

watches from over my shoulders
guiding me along this bumpy road.
I am not who you think I am.
I am not who you think I am.
I am a reflection
of what you want me to be.
I am what I hold.
  your
      hand
    body
      soul.
and still here I remain
on the edge of the bed
as the crackles and screams from the pipes
keep me company
during these winter mornings.
i've searched forever
and
inspiration comes and goes…
but when she is with me,
it is the sweetness of nectar.
just one more day
 and i will wash
these hands
and
maybe ,
i   don't   know
   try again
            at another day.

american standard (#27)

And so
i return to where it all began
as some lonesome traveler
like kerouac and cassidy
like butch and the kid
running away
to simply
catch up to where i left off.
i am the struggle
i am the fighter
i am the dreamer
i am
        the struggle.
with callous hands
and a bad back,
trying to find my keys
cause the job starts at 3
and i'm running late
it's only been 2 weeks of work
yet it feels like a lifetime.
i been running hard all these years
against conforming
against the masses
against settling
but it has caught up to me
in the last lap of the race.
And so,
i return to the start
daylight savings ends
grey fills these days
black fills these nights
but the standards remain the same
in this battle of evermore,
just as i thought they would.

love stays within and yet still without
and i miss your voice.
the drink remains on the stove
from a late last night.
as the broken dreams of angels
and morning rain
                    settles itself,
as a sad song
              on fall days;
for the pure of heart & mind.
i am
where
 i always wanted to be,
only
it's not what i thought.
but these dreams must count for something.
all that sits within me as some restless beast
must stand a chance
for what lies behind the front door.

american standard (#28)

I owe this one to myself
And myself alone.
As I continue down this road
Sometimes lonesome,
Sometimes filled to capacity
For me,
I never wanted a ford
My father had one
But got rid of it for a Jeep
And so shall I do the same
But for now
I walk
Like those before me
And all those to follow
I don't know what will come of this anymore
Yet at some point I did
Or thought I did.
The street corners aren't the same
Landscape changed
Just as the view from this window
And this life has grown again
Still hoping that I'm closer to the answer
Even though I've forgot the question
Wondering what will become of me
Of you
Of him and her
Knowing that it really doesn't matter
Especially at 3.40 a.m.
The questionable hour
of night and day
begging for a smoke to break the stillness

while the drunken kids bicker over
who can drink the most.
I'm trying to give up the smoke now too
Curb the drinking
Read more sleep more work more
Fighting to the death
Trying to be the hero in a Hemingway novel
The last man standing
I forget the word right now,
But you know what I mean.
And still
And still
This hearts beats evermore for understanding
Just as a child
    Just like an old man.

finis.

(for the moment.)

www.ingramcontent.com/pod-product-compliance
Lightning Source LLC
Chambersburg PA
CBHW061726020426
42331CB00006B/1113